CW01207232

I READ! YOU READ!

Child's Turn to Read

Adult's Turn to Read

WE READ ABOUT
The Indian Ocean

By Lauren Gordon and Madison Parker

Table of Contents

The Indian Ocean	3
Words to Know	22
Index	23
Comprehension Questions	23

SEAHORSE PUBLISHING

Parent and Caregiver Guide

Reading aloud with your child has many benefits. It expands vocabulary, sparks discussion, and promotes an emotional bond. Research shows that children who have books read aloud to them have improved language skills, leading to greater school success.

I Read! You Read! books offer a fun and easy way to read with your child. Follow these guidelines.

Before Reading

- Look at the front and back covers. Discuss personal experiences that relate to the topic.
- Read the *Words to Know* at the back of the book. Talk about what the words mean.
- If the book will be challenging or unfamiliar to your child, read it aloud by yourself the first time. Then, invite your child to participate in a second reading.

During Reading

CHILD Have your child read the words beside this symbol. This text has been carefully matched to the reading and grade levels shown on the cover.

ADULT You read the words beside this symbol.

- Stop often to discuss what you are reading and to make sure your child understands.
- If your child struggles with decoding a word, help them sound it out. If it is still a challenge, say the word for your child and have them repeat it after you.
- To find the meaning of a word, look for clues in the surrounding words and pictures.

After Reading

- Praise your child's efforts. Notice how they have grown as a reader.
- Use the *Comprehension Questions* at the back of the book.
- Discuss what your child learned and what they liked or didn't like about the book.

Most importantly, let your child know that reading is fun and worthwhile. Keep reading together as your child's skills and confidence grow.

The Indian Ocean

There are five oceans on Earth.

One is the Indian Ocean.

Oceans are giant bodies of salt water.

CHILD

The Indian Ocean is found between southern Asia, Africa, and Australia.

ADULT

Over 70 percent of Earth's surface is covered by oceans. Of the five oceans on Earth, the Indian Ocean is the youngest.

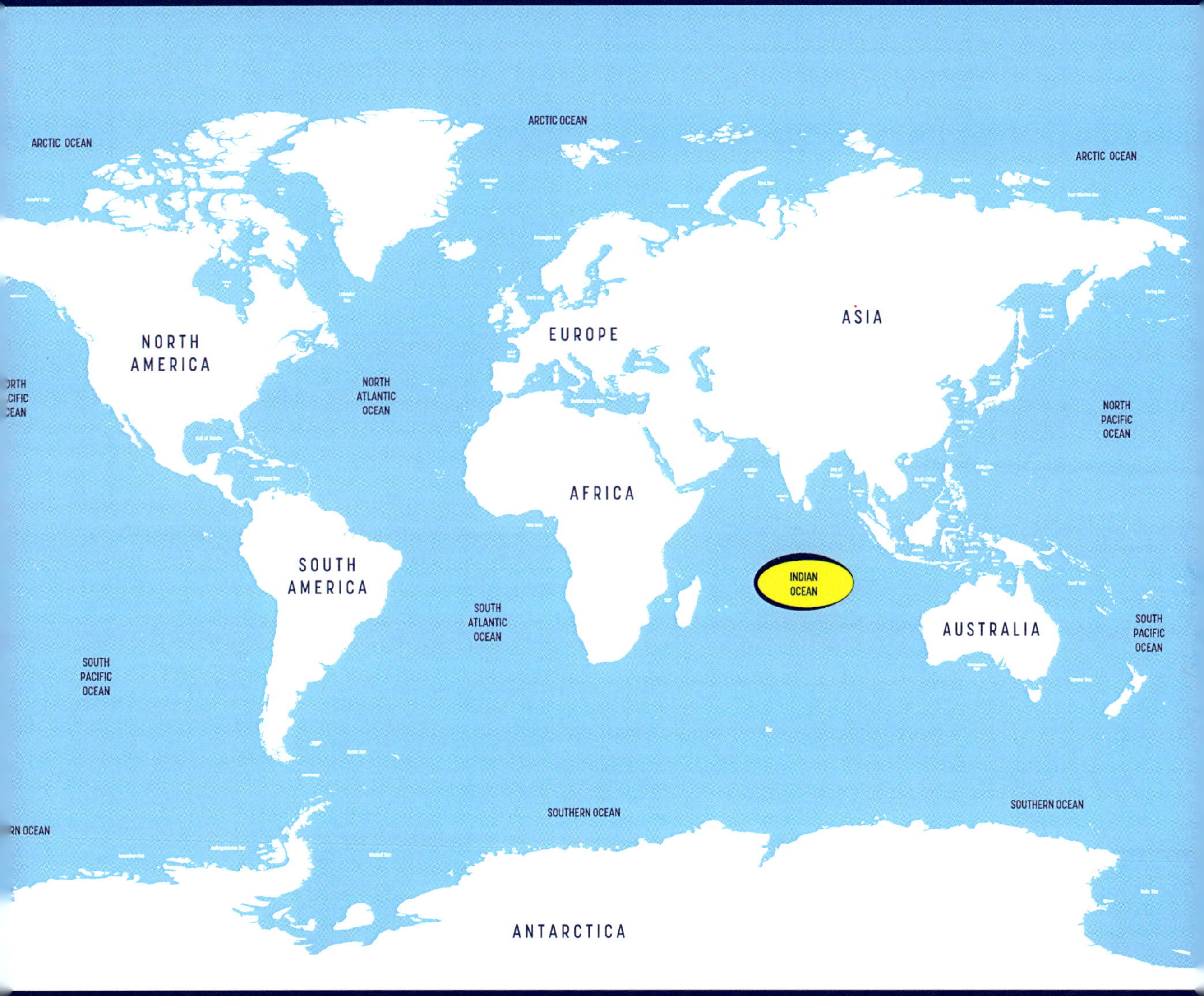
ARCTIC OCEAN
ARCTIC OCEAN
ARCTIC OCEAN
NORTH AMERICA
EUROPE
ASIA
NORTH ATLANTIC OCEAN
NORTH PACIFIC OCEAN
AFRICA
SOUTH AMERICA
INDIAN OCEAN
SOUTH ATLANTIC OCEAN
AUSTRALIA
SOUTH PACIFIC OCEAN
SOUTH PACIFIC OCEAN
SOUTHERN OCEAN
SOUTHERN OCEAN
ANTARCTICA

There are many **islands** in the Indian Ocean.

Some of them are Madagascar and Sri Lanka.

Hundreds of tiny islands make up the country of Maldives.

Sri Lanka and the Maldives are in Asia. Madagascar, the biggest **island** in the Indian Ocean, is part of Africa.

Lemurs live only in Madagascar.

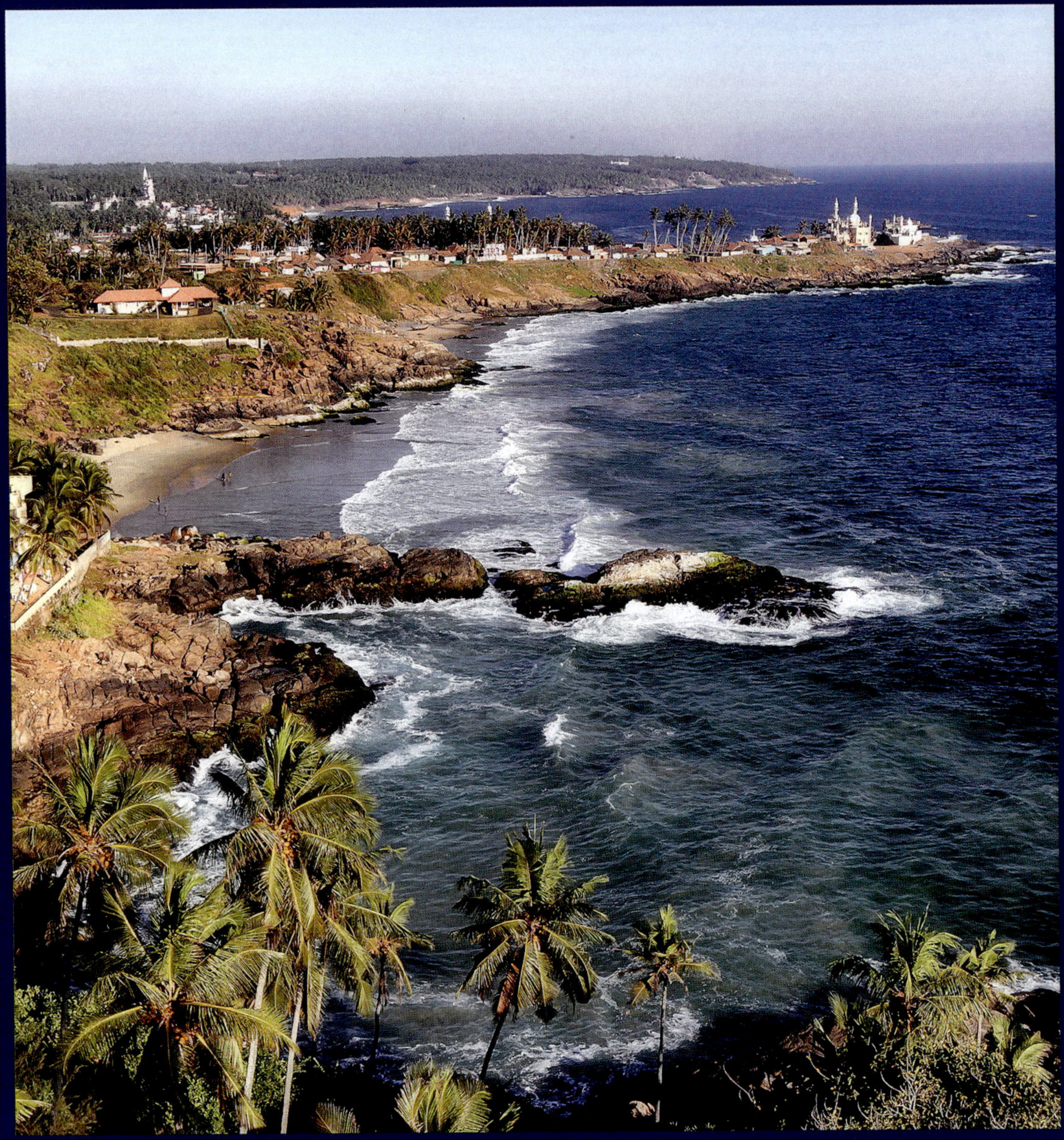

The Indian Ocean got its name from the nearby country of India.

India **protrudes** into the Indian Ocean.

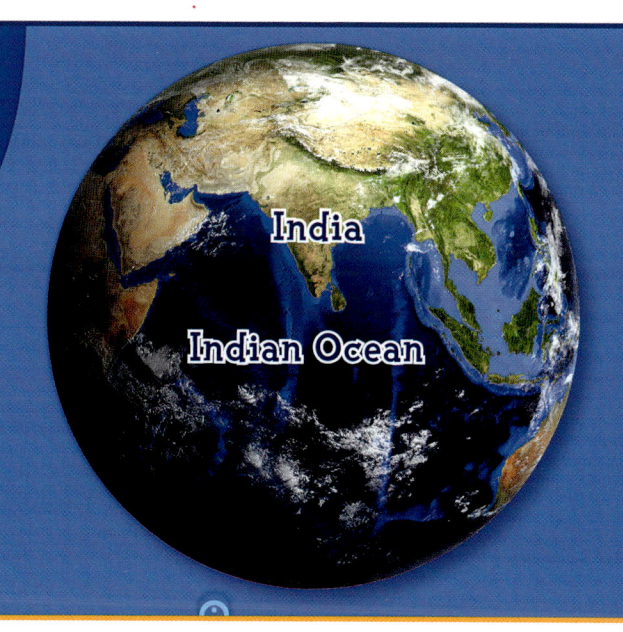

India is a country on the continent of Asia. The Indian Ocean got its name in the year 1515.

The Indian Ocean is the third biggest ocean in the world.

It is about the same size as five and a half United States of Americas put together!

The Indian Ocean stretches for 6,200 miles (10,000 kilometers) between the continents of Africa and Australia.

United States

Indian Ocean

The Indian Ocean is very deep.

It can be up to 23,000 feet (7,000 meters) deep.

That is over five miles (eight kilometers) deep!

CHILD

Oceans have three major layers. The sunlight zone, at the top, gets light and heat from the sun. The twilight zone, in the middle, is darker and colder. The midnight zone, at the bottom, is always dark and cold.

ADULT

13

The Indian Ocean is the warmest ocean in the world.

Warm waters make the Indian Ocean **vulnerable** to cyclones, tsunamis, and strong storms.

Cyclones are like tornadoes, but they are made of water. Tsunamis are huge waves of water. A deadly tsunami from the Indian Ocean hit land in 2004.

A tsunami is a giant, destructive wave caused by an earthquake under the sea.

15

CHILD

The Indian Ocean's coral reefs are important **ecosystems**.

Laws protect coral reefs near Africa and Australia.

ADULT

Coral are tiny animals. Their shells make reefs that provide habitats for many animals. Coral reefs support 25 percent of life in the ocean.

Thousands of species, or types, of fish and other ocean animals live in coral reefs.

CHILD

Leatherback turtles live in the Indian Ocean.

Because of hunting and **pollution**, they are now **endangered**.

ADULT

Leatherbacks can swim to depths of about 4,000 feet (1,220 meters). This helps them look for prey and avoid predators.

The leatherback turtle is the largest sea turtle and one of the biggest reptiles on Earth.

19

CHILD

The Indian Ocean is in danger.

It is changing as ice melts at Earth's polar caps.

ADULT

Using less plastic and conserving water are two ways to help the Indian Ocean. How will you help protect this special body of water?

Earth's polar caps are at the North and South Poles.

North Pole

South Pole

21

Words to Know

ecosystems (EE-koh-sis-tuhms): communities of living things, including plants and animals, that share an environment

endangered (en-DAYN-jurd): threatened; in danger of becoming extinct

islands (EYE-luhnds): pieces of land completely surrounded by water

pollution (puh-LOO-shuhn): harmful materials that damage air, water, and soil, including gases, chemicals, and smoke

protrudes (proh-TROODZ): sticks out into

vulnerable (VUHL-nur-uh-buhl): weak and without protection

Index

continent(s) 3, 4, 5, 9, 10
ecosystems 16
endangered 18
India 9

leatherback turtles 18
pollution 18
size 10
tsunami(s) 14

Comprehension Questions

1. True or False: The Indian Ocean is one of three oceans in the world.

2. True or False: There are many islands in the Indian Ocean.

3. True or False: The Indian Ocean is the coldest ocean.

4. True or False: The Indian Ocean is home to the leatherback turtle.

5. True or False: The Indian Ocean is named after the country of India.

Answers
1. False 2. True 3. False 4. True 5. True

Written by: Lauren Gordon and Madison Parker
Design by: Jen Bowers
Editor: Kim Thompson

Library of Congress PCN Data
We Read About the Indian Ocean / Lauren Gordon and Madison Parker
I Read! You Read!
ISBN 979-8-8873-5197-1 (hard cover)
ISBN 979-8-8873-5217-6 (paperback)
ISBN 979-8-8873-5237-4 (EPUB)
ISBN 979-8-8873-5257-2 (eBook)
Library of Congress Control Number: 2022945532

Printed in the United States of America.

Photographs from Shutterstock.com: Cover and p.17 image ©2015 V_E, backgound ©2012 Andrey_Kuzmin, water globe ©2012 zffoto; p.2 and throughout backgroud ©elic; p.3 and throughout background ©Aleksandra Bataeva, globes ©Designua; p.5 ©Pyty; p.7 ©2017 Hajakely, ©2014 javarman; p.8 ©2020 Dzerkach Viktar; p.9 ©2012 ixpert; p.11 ©2008 Alex Staroseltsev, ©2017 Harvepino; p.13 ©2021 Martin Prochazkacz; p.15 ©2013 IgorZh; p.19 ©2020 Giovanny Gava; p.21 ©2009 Intrepix

Seahorse Publishing Company
www.seahorsepub.com

Copyright © 2023 **SEAHORSE PUBLISHING COMPANY**

All rights reserved. No part of this publication may be reproduced, stored in a retrieval system or be transmitted in any form or by any means, electronic, mechanical, photocopying, recording, or otherwise, without the prior written permission of Seahorse Publishing Company.

Published in the United States
Seahorse Publishing
PO Box 771255
Coral Springs, FL 33077